MW00982286

DO NOT CALL ME BY MY NAME

Cataloguing In Publication (CIP) data for this book is available through The Canadian CIP Program coordinated by Library and Archives Canada.

ISBN 978-0-88753-491-1

Design: Kate Hargreaves

Black Moss Press

EST. 1969

Published by Black Moss Press at 2450 Byng Road, Windsor, Ontario, N8W 3E8 Canada. Black Moss books are distributed in Canada and the U.S. by LitDistCo. All orders should be directed there.

Black Moss Press books can also be found on our website www.blackmosspress.com.

Black Moss would like to acknowledge the generous financial support from both the Canada Council of the Arts and the Ontario Arts Council.

Canada Council   Conseil des Arts
for the Arts   du Canada

ONTARIO ARTS COUNCIL
CONSEIL DES ARTS DE L'ONTARIO

PRINTED IN CANADA

DO NOT CALL ME
BY MY NAME

LISA SHATZKY

Black Moss
2011 Press

CONTENTS

ACKNOWLEDGEMENTS

My gratitude to the Glenairley Poets in Sooke, B.C. and the Rivendell Poets, on Bowen Island, B.C. for their friendship and support of my work over many years. I am deeply appreciative of Patrick Lane, mentor and friend, and it is through him I have learned so much about how poetry sings. Thank you to my dear Wendy Morton for her laughter and keen eyes. Thank you to my colleagues in the therapy world who heard earlier drafts of these poems. And thank you to Marty Gervais of Black Moss Press and his editors Jessica Minervini and Susie Boldt-Heinrichs for believing in this work. And to my children, with deepest love, Jordyne, Benji, and Jonah, for their gracious tolerance of a mother as poet. You are my greatest inspiration. Thank you also to Sam Greenspoon. Finally, thank you to Don MacLean, whose love for me and my poems has allowed me to soar, for indeed his words, "you are the poems and the poems are you" have brought me to heights I could not have imagined.

INTRODUCTION

This collection of forty poems *Do Not Call Me by My Name* is dedicated to all of Canada's First Nations' people who suffered at the hands of the Canadian Government's Residential School System of the not so distant past. My work as a trauma therapist has brought me into contact with First Nations communities along British Columbia's Southern and Northern coasts for the past seventeen years. Through the course of my work with these communities, I have listened to their stories and been inspired by their resilience and incredible sense of spirit. It has been a great privilege to work with the children and youth and to help them find their way amongst the terrible loss and grief that their parents and grandparents carry. Such is the essence of the multigenerational trauma that still exists in these communities.

All names and identifying information have been changed to maintain confidentiality. But the poems speak of what has happened to these children and they force us head-on into the pathos, the overwhelming beauty, the sense of unbearable loss. As we read on, the only cushioning restraints are the beauty of language, the aesthetic and emotional impact of poetry.

Perhaps these poems have been my way to honour the brave and courageous journeys of the generations that continue to struggle to survive. These are terrible and sad poems, but they are also human and necessary. They speak the unspeakable. But somewhere in the ashes, there is grief that gives life...that transcends.

lisa shatzky
Bowen Island, B.C.

CHILDREN LOST

What do I do with their faces,
the faces of those children
whose stories have entered me
by chance, like the small rain
of a coastal forest in early spring?
I see them in the light that breathes
and knits the leaves their colours.
I hear them when the moon falls
on nights luminous and transparent
and weeping in my hands.

The boy who witnessed his father
French kissing the barrel of a gun
then swallowing what was inside.
The girl not held for two years
until all sound was extinguished
from her body.
The one with the auburn curls
too eager to show the cigarette burns
on ivory thighs.
The pale teen who pretends to be "Goth"
and finds more solace in the arms

of her pimp
than in the home of her father
who creeps into her room each night.
These are the things I think of now:
their hands, soft and dimpled,
for only so long.
Their baby teeth; did anyone notice
when they were gone?
Their eyes, once wide and wondrous
meadows where bright spirits played. And
their laughter. Their laughter.
Their laughter.
I would kill for their laughter's return.
Instead I weep.
I weep with the moon
falling into the dark.

THEY DIDN'T SEE ALICE FALL

Some things fall and cannot be caught.
They spiral down from some place
you cannot imagine. Like moonlight
sifting through mist, unseen
at first, but out of the corner
of your eye there it is, quivering
the window's edge.
They didn't see Alice
until the fall had already picked up
such speed, a meteor
hurling through space
getting faster and faster as it gets closer
to crashing. It was too late
when they noticed her.
Her life already broken and splattered
into pieces no one could imagine,
No one could reach.

IF THESE TREES COULD SPEAK

If these trees could speak
they would tell you things
you would never understand.
How it's possible to love your kids
and still lose your way with them.
How everyone here is in pain.
Those who came before us.
Only wounded people wound people.
From the outside it just looks
like some fucked up people.
But come closer.
Come closer.
Look inside.
Listen, listen.
There is music here.
Even in the pain and sadness,
there is music.
holding us together.

MY BROTHER'S WINGS

I want to wrap my arms around you
dear brother and fly my way out of town.
I want to see you grinning again,
that beautiful savage grin of yours
as you tried to fly
like a wild bird soaring
into an ominous ocean of sky.
And I am flying with you, my brother,
your small taunt body flexing for the wind,
unstoppable hair in the face,
flying away
from the roadside shrine
that grew and blossomed after you jumped.

I want to fly away from the sunflowers
someone planted.
Your baseball jersey
carefully laid out on a log,
and all your trophies.
I want to fly away from our mother
and the nightmare she now carries inside.
A despair that will eventually cripple her,

seep into her body like a slow poison
as she dies your death over and over again.
And here words will fail us terribly.
They are broken street lamps blinking
on and off like useless prayers.
Summer vanishes before it arrives.

MY GRANDFATHER'S FRIEND

He would never tell us
what happened at the residential school.
He cried when we asked questions.
But one day he told us about his friend.
He found him in a field one night,
a boy no more than ten
with his head spilling into the earth.
A beautiful boy, eyes still
open and lips
in the shape of a kiss.
He spoke of sitting beside him
through the night,
taking his hand
under a perfect sky
bleeding stars and dust and lost dreams
and waiting,
waiting for something
that would never
come.

Somewhere in a field
there is a boy
my grandfather never left.
The one thing he allowed us

to carry with him.
And we did
and still do
and see the boy everywhere.
We offer small fragments
of songs
found
in the rain.

DREAMS

I wish my mother
would not always have wet eyes.
I wish my father
was around to kiss me good-night.
I wish my sister
would tell me silly jokes again
when we used to have pillow fights.
I wish my grandma
didn't smell like medicine.
I wish my grandpa
could stand up without shaking
and not keep falling down.
I wish someone
would see
how my little heart
cannot cry.
It has become so hard.
Please help me
make my heart
soft again.

THE EARTH WEEPS

The Earth weeps for all of us.
We think we need to save her.
But the Earth knows more
than we do about life.
The Earth knows how to heal herself.
She can fill in the holes
and turn herself into something new.
We are not able to do that.
We are always returning to what happened to us.
We can't seem to get out of the holes.
They swallow us,
fill us with dark
and keep us small.
But we need
to be larger.
To fill ourselves with light.
The Earth weeps for us.
Everywhere there is light.
If only we could reach it.

DO NOT CALL ME BY MY NAME

THE ELDERS

My grandfather does not
speak about the past.
I used to wonder
what it was like in the days
when they took the children away.
Once I asked him
to tell me his story.
His eyes swelled
like big blue mountains
and he could not speak.
Then the mountains broke
and rivers streamed
down his face.
I never asked again.
I understood.
When you take away
a people's children,
the elders lose
their stories.

POISON

You can't know
the pain of this place.
The flowers still grow
but sometimes,
like the children,
they grow strangely.
The pain of this place has poisoned them.
Sometimes the children's eyes stay closed.
Sometimes they can't talk,
they can't move,
their legs don't want to walk.
The grown-ups don't know what to do.
They too
were poisoned
long ago.

DO NOT CALL ME BY MY NAME

Childhood was a room
I wandered into by mistake
and could not find my way out.
It was like having years
of keys and none of them
opening the door.

I don't remember anything
growing in that room,
only the way the sun disappeared
early, staring out the window
and not being surprised
by the fullness
of absence.

So do not come looking
for me here.
Do not call me
by my name.
You might find the shell
that once held pearls,
or the vase of the dead yellow

rose in the window,
but these are tricks of light,
what you see
what you don't.
I once was among the cardboard
dolls with their paper clothes
and permanent smiles
but I am no longer there.
I am the burning wild grass
through melting snow.
I am the wailing
of the midnight herons.
I am the long melodic sound
a turtle makes
when it dies.
I am the dew drop
on the morning's breath.

Do not call me
by my name.
I am not singular.
I am all the children who drowned.
I am all the children who could not speak,
and the ones who learned to fly
and all the ones who found their way back,
through the thistle and the thorns,
through the abandoned years
and wasted scraps of memory,
carrying a pail full of blackberries
for the first time
at last.

BETTY'S TINY SPARROWS

You keep returning
to that place in the dark bosom
of sea, that island,
disguised in fog
shrouded softness that never lifts.
She is there
small and awkward,
though you can't find her.
But her eyes and voice awaken you most nights
and the scars on her delicate wrists
still sing.
Your hands once held those scars
like tiny sparrows that would not be caged.
You remember how they tried to fly away.
She used to hum while she danced on the kitchen floor
as the autumn light turned her hair into gold.
You shared ghost stories by the winter fire.
She laughed when you ran from spiders.
You can still hear her laughter.
A rustling in the leaves.
To catch the moon
when it falls.

THE RIVER WHERE YOU DROWNED

I come back to the field
by the river, thirsty
and looking for truth
in the half light of a scarred moon.
Instead, there is a rusting lantern full
of holes, found among the foxgloves
spilling themselves and the cries
of the midnight herons.
The fullness of absence
and the absence of fullness
keep us wanting
to pin things down.
To hold what will eventually leave us.
I keep pieces of you
in a box under the bed.
Your eyeglasses.
The dried lavender.
A small hunting knife never used.
I still try to pull a few last truths
from the river you drowned in,
and if I could, I would paste them in a scrapbook
for comfort on those windy nights.
But they dissolve at the touch of my hands.
Tricks of light.

DO NOT CALL ME BY MY NAME

What is here, what is not.
Only a child remains, small and vital, standing by.
The water's cold grasp.
Wild lavender in her arms.

Why can't she see me? How long
before she falls?

BLACKBERRIES

Finally, rain.
Soft drumming on the roof
and in the arms of trees.
No matter how much you rehearse this, you are never ready.
The wind scatters the seeds too early.
And the fallen maple leaves
rusted from their lives
offer red and gold.
Somewhere a tree frog.
A midnight owl.
Even in grief there is song.
Even when pieces of the heart
are broken and taken

the heart carries on.
In a fog shrouded inlet there is a girl
trying to find her way home.
Carrying a pail for the blackberries
that never got picked.
I want to write my way back to her,
back to the darkness that washed over the day
and the pail she never let go of.
I want to tell her
that music is what holds

together this confusion,
that here in the open spaces
between the words,
here along the edges
where the cedars still sing,
are the blackberries
we missed
the first time around.

I IMAGINE A SWING

We come across that old photograph
of the red brick house in the snow.
The year of the blizzard.
The snow is as high as the roof on one side
and what remains of the porch is a vague impression.
A bare maple tree leans toward the house.
I imagine a swing but there is no swing
in the photograph.
Instead the house looks as if it might sink.

Spring was just around the corner, you insist
and point to something that is supposed to be
the lilac bush starting to bud.
I don't see a lilac bush, only a smudged blotch.
But if I look closely, squint a little,
I can see a boy's face in the upstairs window.
He stares out with orange gold eyes,
like kumquat fruit in the wrong season.
I trace my fingers over the boy's mouth,
touch his eyes gingerly.
They are blurred, out of focus.
I can't tell if it's the age of the photograph
or a trick of light.
I caress his forehead where the hair used to fall.
You do not see the boy.
You cannot see him.
Instead you speak of songbirds,
how they nested in the backyard.
I remember the sparrows
singing fractured
prayers.

But we are more migratory
than sparrows
and carry our bruised
silences like stones.

Sometimes the stones
fall, by accident, they slip
from our mouths and for a moment
we are free.
We do cartwheels in the dark
and carve holes in the ice,
we quarrel with memory and bring back the sun
and the seasons and the swings

and we become children
many years after the fact.

DESCENDING

Falling.
Into the sinkhole again.
The dark funnel shaped crack in the limestone.
Going about your day and everything
slipping out of your hands.
And the world becomes flatter
and the trees and buildings collapse,
colours ooze out of their jars
until only a hard crust remains.
The sky blurs then erases the stars,
the ground liquidates until eventually you are floating
somewhere, suspended in slow motion
watching your life happen without you.
People talking and you can't understand a word
because they are talking too fast or too slow.
Waiting for the phone to ring
and no one calls for days
and no emails arrive
and you keep checking
checking and wandering
around the house in your underwear
eating peanut butter from the jar

with your fingers and unable to decide
if it's morning or if it's night.

What's most frightening
is that there is nothing you
wouldn't do to bring yourself back.
Gleefully slash your skin just to feel
the warmth of your blood.

Colour your hair purple. Then pink.
Then cut it all off. Then spend the day
in bed with the curtains drawn
mourning your hair.
Stand in the middle of a busy
intersection and see if anyone
hits you. Bring it on, you scream
in the loud silences of your mind,
Bring it on.

But even the cars pass you by.

JAYNE WHO LOVES THE MOON

You know what you have to do
to survive in this house.
Smile green meadows
and blink soft flowers
and pretend you don't know.
Pretend to be an imbecile, harmless
and dancing on the cracked linoleum floor.
Humming to music only you can hear.
No fear, no horror in your eyes, only simple blinking,
miniature black moons that show nothing.
Pretend you don't notice him
slithering into your sister's room at night.
Pretend you can't see your mother's sunken eyes,
decaying lakes that dried up long ago.
Pretend your feet are the pattering
of a small animal scratching,
digging, burrowing
a way out.

DO NOT CALL ME BY MY NAME

BOY OF THE RAVENS

I hate you, says the boy
and grabs the man's leg.
I'll protect you, says the man
and shoves the boy away.
Please don't leave me, weeps the boy
and throws his fists at the man.
Pull yourself together says the man
spitting on the ground.
I'm scared, says the boy glaring.
Be a big boy, says the man
lighting up a cigarette.
I hate you, I hate you, whispers the boy.
You loved it, says the man
and offers the boy a drag.
I still hate you, says the boy
taking the cigarette and coughing.
You're okay, says the man
and turns to walk away.
Don't leave me, yells the boy.
The man smiles.

LUCY WHO DREAMED OF NEW ORLEANS

It would have been more clear
had he used his fists.
At least I would have known what was happening.
But his way was subtle, the sun's rays
before they burn.

I couldn't see beyond the promised vistas,
blue and silver mountains singing.
I couldn't see how I became the lamb
hanging upside down in the marketplace
slowly bleeding out.
Perspective is hard from this angle.
Everything swirling, laughter and colours and trinkets
as if in a carnival.

(They say at the Carnival in New Orleans
women earn beads by flashing their breasts
at strangers. It's all part of the fun)

That's what I think of now
though I've never been to New Orleans.
I've never been off this coast.
Never past Prince Rupert.
But I think of New Orleans and the Carnival.

DO NOT CALL ME BY MY NAME

As if it can explain something
that can't be explained
on a stained grey mattress
in a basement
where I snorted whatever was offered
in exchange for a few small thrills
and what love could be imagined.

THEY CALL HER MORNING SUN

On a bed that is not her own
she closes her eyes
and knows not to struggle
but to play dead.
He is gentler with her this way.
She allows the maps of her body
to be travelled with his leather
tongue and sandpaper hands
glistening small streams
running down her cheeks.
His breath smells sour
and there's that strange clicking
sound he makes with his mouth.
It makes her sick.
If she gags he'll push her roughly to the floor
and call her names
whore bitch cunt
she's heard them all
and knows what they mean.
She is eight years old.

I WANTED TO BELIEVE WE WERE HAPPY

It's not what you think.
The kitchen was warm
with the smell of something cooking.
One of those apple crisps.
Or chocolate chip cookies.
You would never know anything was wrong.
It was not one of those houses you read about.
See the school pictures
on the table by the door.
We were happy children.
I wanted to believe we were happy.
Our family helped the other families.
We loved the old traditions.
And the new modern ways.
It was a beautiful house.
See the African violets
exclaiming purple by the window.
The living room sofa cushions
matching the curtains, gold and auburn.
Such symmetry.
Such precision.
The house and all its trappings.
The games room. Xbox and plasma television.
We wanted to be there.

To be the happy family in the photos.
Laughing.
See that one with the missing teeth.
Smiling without a care in the world.
You would never know
that was the year it started.
The games room.

JONNIE WHO BECAME A WOLF

How do you tell them about the babysitter
who comes into your dreams,
when you are dreaming
of that special beach in Sootka Sound?
What you remember most about that beach
is the way the waves catch the light
and a thousand suns
dance in your eyes.
The suns are so bright
you can hardly keep your eyes open.
He is standing there
with his pants down in front of you.
You're sitting in the warm sand
and have no words for what he's doing there.
No one else sees him.
Children laughing and your grandmother
offering you a tuna sandwich
and your little brother
burying his toys in the sand
and asking you to find them.
Touch it, says the babysitter
and you turn away and stare

at the sand and the picnic basket
and your grandmother's orange sunhat.
You stare at the bright beach towels,
especially the one that has the wolves howling
to the moon and you think if you stare
long enough you can become one of them,
one of those wolves on the beach towel.
And they will call you the boy who became a wolf.
And you will forget everything.
Everything that happened.
But how do you tell them
he keeps finding you,
even here, in your dreams, in the corners
of your eyes you can still see him standing there.
How do you speak of it
when everyone is smiling and happy
and the waves hold a thousand
suns?

ANTHONY LOVED THE WHALES

And one day you don't cry.
The tears do not come.
Everything still feels the same,
the heart with its gaping holes,
the lungs burning from all that breathing under water,
but the tears are gone.
Just like the whales you loved.
You haven't seen any whales in a long time.
They just disappeared
when you weren't looking.
Like in early winter when suddenly the lake freezes over
and you realize it's colder than you thought
and you're still wearing a t-shirt outside.
But ice has its advantages.
You can now skate
where you once had to walk.
It's faster on skates.
You can do circles and spin and twirl
and carve your name in the hardness.
You feel like a dare devil now.
One of those power rangers.
A ninja turtle.

You wouldn't try those stunts on a soft surface,
the moonlight spilling
and gushing itself everywhere,
and all that light
going nowhere.

MARIA HEARS THE FLOWER

The almost audible breathing
of the lone flower in the basement.
She is the only one who can hear it
and goes to water it sometimes.
There in the dark it grows.
In a corner in a crack
in the cement floor where a slit
of light slips through the piece of window
not yet boarded up.
A small something finds the small slice of light
and reaches toward it.
She doesn't know how long
it has been there or why.
But as long as a flower
pushes through the hard surface
she will keep listening for it.
Sometimes it only takes a flower
to give enough reason for the heart
to carry on.

THE ONE THEY CALLED THE LITTLE MAN

He stands
on Lions Gate bridge and the wind
does not disappoint him.
The sun bright and the mountains
yawning snow.
This is how he imagined it would be.
The perfect day for the perfect dive.
He thinks of her smell, her breasts, the unholiness
of their interwoven flesh.
Her long familiar fingers. Her lips.
His Ecstasy. His Nightmare.
They are one. She made him this way.
Her little man.
When the big man took off
with some white woman from the school.
He took the torch she handed him.
Hands shaking. Heart pounding.
And she took him in.
To satin sheets and lavender massage oils.
To black lace and blood red painted toenails.
To wine and vodka so he could relax.
She said human bodies are natural and nothing

DO NOT CALL ME BY MY NAME

to be ashamed of.
He believed her.
He couldn't think about anything else.
And he hated himself and hated her
and hungrily drank the sweet poison
she offered.
Here high above
the wanting hands of the sea,
he will turn himself into a bird
that can no longer see anything
but the blue above him
and the blue below
and they are the same.
The kind of blue he will give himself to
one last time,
the same colour as his mother's eyes
before the poison,
before he couldn't stop himself
for reaching for more.
Before he could no longer remember
what colour her eyes
used to be.

ANDY THE SONGWRITER

He spills his life
out of a green knapsack:
six condoms, two comic books, a yellow hoodie,
grey socks, a broken ipod, cigarettes,
an expired bus pass, what's left of a joint.
A few jelly beans fall out. A notebook
folded and torn. A crushed beer can.
He's looking for that cd of a song
he recorded to show the therapist
that he's not as screwed up as they say,
that he still can make something
warm, something almost beautiful.
A song that tells the story of who he was
when he once had wings
and knew how to fly.

JESSICA THE WARRIOR

She smiles widely
as she walks by the construction workers.
At thirteen she knows
how far a smile can take her.
What doors breasts will open.
What roads the hips can travel
and how skin alone
stretches the truth
until you no longer know
what actually happened
and what it is you tell yourself
so that you can keep doing what you do
and not feel anything.
You learn not to feel.
Life is easier that way.
The hips swinging, opening,
closing, opening, closing,
just enough to lull the men
into a deep sleep
as they stop to watch
her walking by and she can feel them drooling
like rabid dogs in a desert

that would kill as easily as fuck.
A difference
she herself no longer
knows.

MICHAEL JR OF THE THUNDERBIRDS

He wonders if they can tell
that no one lives here anymore.
The house looks okay from a distance
but up close the peeled paint and the sinking
deck are telltale signs.
Bulbs were planted once
but one cold winter rotted most of them.
Now no flowers grow.
A window is shattered,
another boarded up.
No one has even bothered
to decorate the boarded up one
with graffiti singing political passions
and proverbs about fucking.
Only the sun degrades the house now.

Still, the surveyors gather around
with their shovels and measuring tape
thinking something can be done.
They are optimists.
They believe in the power of restoration.

Just like his social workers.
They think something can be done.
Let's connect you back to your culture
they say over and over again.
But it's too late for that.
They don't know about the rotting
flesh under the boards and glass,
the heart that barely moves.

And all the wasted blood.
He knows that what you see
is no longer what you get.

SOCIAL WORKERS

The lady asking questions
has eyes that look like they are about to overflow
with all the rivers of the mountains,
the spring run-off where you grew up
near the Koeye River on the Northern Coast
and you haven't yet said a word.
Her eyes are blue skies you could lose yourself in,
if it wasn't still dark winter.
She holds documents
in her hands and they flap
like the wings of white birds as she speaks.
She can't keep the birds still,
they are flapping and fluttering
in the breath of her words
and you can't decipher what she is saying.
She says you will feel better
if you express your feelings.
You stare at the paper doves
in her hands and want to fly
away with them.
You want to break her hands, slit her wrists
so that all the paper doves

will fall to the ground.
Maybe a few will learn to fly.

She says you must express your feelings.
But there's nothing left to say
once you've seen your father kill your mother
and your brother fuck your sister.
You can tell just by the way
she holds those doves
in her tight white fists
that she knows nothing
about these kinds of things.
The same tight white fists
that built the residential schools
and stole your parents from you
before you were even born.

BETHANY OF THE BEES

He calls it her little "we".
Where the bees live.
He brushes her hair
and buys her those fancy gold lollipops.
A "we" for the bees so the flowers can grow.
And all the bees can dance.
She imagines them coming to the flowers.
All those bees.
She's not supposed to tell anyone
of their secret meadow.
Of how he taught them to dance.
Sometimes she puts her hands down there
to feel them, to make sure they're still alive.
Like he showed her.
She doesn't tell anyone.
Some things are private.
Some things only grandpas know about.
She goes to the place
he showed her
to make sure the bees are still there.
Still there.

KAYLA IN THE WINDOW

The yellow rose in the window;
when you first come into the room,
it looks perfect.
The light illuminates the yellow
like summer mornings,
like endless days.
It sits in an antique blue vase
with clear water at the base of the stem.
The water never changes.
The rose never opens.
It's perfect and closed.
Pursed lips.
Where the sun touches the stem in the afternoon,
there is a cut on one side, almost invisible,
only seen in a certain light.
What was liquid inside is now as hard as glue.
It glistens.
Sometimes it sings.
A screeching kind of song,
a siren in the light.
Like her left side.
It sings the siren song.

DO NOT CALL ME BY MY NAME

Where he held the knife.
As he opened her.
As he turned what was soft
into something hard.
But from the outside
she looks perfect.
Closed.

KENDRA THE CELEBRITY

Her online pictures;
her friends can't keep their eyes off them.
They tag them on facebook.
Swoon over laptops in the school cafeteria.
Text message each other.
She has become a celebrity.
But she just laughs and shrugs
and says it was no big deal.
She doesn't tell them how hard
his hands were.
The dead city in her stomach.
Street lights shattered
and garbage everywhere.
That is where she now lives.
Where the lilies once bloomed
are black pits where anything
and everything bad comes from.
Decaying black pits.
Her eyes.
Her stomach,
But they like her online pictures.
She is a celebrity.

DANNY'S DISAPPEARANCE

He can make himself disappear.
First he must get to the closet.
He brings his sleeping bag, small flashlight,
his boy scout knife.
Once there he closes his eyes
and has to count to ten for each part
he wants to be gone.
It can't happen all at once.
First he must start with his feet
and then work his way up to his head.
It has to go in that order or the disappearing
won't work. Ankles, legs, knees,
until he reaches his eyes,
then at last, his ears.
His ears are always last.
He has to get it right or it can't happen.
He's been practicing for a long time
and knows how to do it right.
But sometimes it doesn't happen fast enough.
Sometimes he runs out of time.
He gets to his head but isn't fast enough
making his ears disappear.

He hears them screaming.
He hears them smashing things.
Walls. Dishes. Doors. Soon slapping.
Punching. Banging. More screaming.
More and more and more. He covers his ears.
But nothing happens.
He can hear everything.
If he doesn't make his ears
disappear in time, he hears.
He hears everything.
Everything.

STEVIE'S LIGHT

He lies awake knowing the footsteps
will soon come.
As long as he sees light under the door
everything is okay.
Maybe tonight will be different.
The moon dances gingerly
on the bedroom floor.
It is summer.
He thinks about baseball and playing
with his friends.
Corn on the cob. Ice cream.
His uncle is going to teach him
to carve soon.
He wants to carve a mask.
Of a big black bear.
So he won't be afraid anymore.
The light under the door begins to fade.
The footsteps are heavy.
Pause.
This part is the most scary.
Waiting. He prays
the footsteps will go away.

In his mind he is already turning
himself into a rock.
His small body is hard.
Untouchable.

FINDING THE CHILD

Eventually you must return
to the house on fire.
Because of a little girl in a blue summer
dress with pink smiling suns
on the sleeves.
The one her mother bought for the party
the day before the girl
fell into the flames.
After all this time, the house
continues to burn.
A burning bush without any god, only a dark
devouring of what might have been.
Whether the house is real or not
depends on who still lives there.
But this time you walk into the fire.
This time, hands and feet blistered,
you breathe in the smoke and the ashes
and the melted dreams
to reach the child.
To finally find what lives,
what has always lived, and bring such life
boldly and unflinchingly back into the open air.

LISA SHATZKY

To leave the burning house and its toxic
truths and boarded-up windows and rotted
past and simply walk away
without looking back.

The child smiling in your arms.

THOMAS OF THE SEA

He lies on his back and watches
the colours come together.
The indigo turns blue then green then yellow pink
yawning into an ocean of sky.
Take me he says in his mind. Take me. Take me.
He is already in the sea, floating away.
Closes his eyes and imagines himself dissolving
into the colours, first his arms, then legs,
then hair, then skin, then bones. then mouth,
all erased, slower then faster, making himself
disappear. He is getting better at it each time.
Sees himself returning to what he was before
he was here, somewhere far away,
somewhere not of this place, not of this earth,
not of this skin, not of this face.
He is the face of the one who stayed,
the one not born, the one who drowned
in the warm dark womb.
When given a choice to emerge, he is the twin
who stayed behind, hands in fists, eyes
tightly closed, he is the one who faded
back into the deep deep sleep of sea
and did not come
into the light.

NELLY WHO LIKED NIETZSCHE QUOTES

It's not so bad.
Your stepfather is good to you.
Unlike the woman who used to be your mother
lying on the couch loaded and oblivious to your name,
let alone what's for dinner.
He cooks all the meals.
Fills out your school forms.
Brings mother tea and hot water bottles.
Extra pillows. His hands are tender.
He tells you his stories. His tears are never-ending
fountains in his eyes.
Tells you he is lonely.
You can't help but feel sorry for him.
To have married into this.
Who can blame him for looking for warmth.
You sit up at night consoling him.
See him as a wounded dog.
A wounded dog who wanders into your room
to share Nietzsche quotes.
You like Nietzsche.
Soon he brings you tea.

Soon you're laughing together.
Soon you're both looking after your mother.
Bringing her soup.
Your finger tips accidently touch his.
He looks at you with wounded wide eyes.
He brushes your hair.
Buys you whatever you want.
Likes your friends.
So what if he lies next to you at night quoting Nietzsche
and holding your breasts.
There are worse things.

SUNSHINE'S MAP

There is an X on a piece of paper I keep
under the bed.
To remind me that I am here.
Like those maps I've seen on hiking trails.
They have a big bold X to tell you where you are.
You are here, the map screams and screams
as if you didn't know.
And you don't.
How can you tell when the gentle forest turns
into a reeking swamp in the blink of an eye.
How can you tell when the trees become shadows
reaching out to grab you like probing fingers
slicing through the mists.
Suddenly the land you thought you were standing on
gives out and you're floating in drifts
of fog and dampness.
You don't know anymore where you are.
The X on the paper is to remind me:
I am here. I am here. I did not die.
I did not disappear. It tried to grab me
but I'm still here.

DO NOT CALL ME BY MY NAME

MARTHA BELIEVES IN FAIRY TALES

She is whatever he wants her to be.
She is made of sand, like the girl
she once read about in a Margaret Atwood poem.
A girl some boys made out of sand
and every afternoon they arrived
thirsting and thrusting into her.
Their bodies crashed through the sand girl's body.
They made her fall apart.
But they rebuilt her afterwards.
Patted her down.
Made her hips wider.
Enlarged her breasts.
She is that girl.
There is nothing left in her that resists.
Her sand body yields to touch, tongue, fingers.
She allows him to dress her in white cashmere sweaters
that make her breasts look like small doves
or black lace to make her legs look like snakes.
He shares her with his friends.

They pay him well.

They compliment her.
And he tells her how beautiful she is,
that she is the princess he has been waiting for
and together they will get rich.
At fifteen she's too old to believe in fairy tales
but it's a nice story and better than the real one;
the one where the father comes in
loaded and sweating
and reaching for his "baby doll".
She'd rather be a princess
than a baby doll.
Any day.

DEREK'S BLOOD RITUALS

He sits in his room with the walls
painted black. The music blaring.
So loud the windows rattle
with the drums.
In his hands an army knife.
He carves long deep lines on his arms.
Criss-cross, over the skull he drew with a pen.
Actually the skull was carved with the pen.
His buddies laughed when the ink

and blood mixed.
Someone said he'd get blood poisoning.
He carried on. What the fuck.
They admire his toughness.
He carves to see the blood.
Letting out what's ready
to explode inside him.
To free what's frozen.
To bring life back into the room.
To not drown.
To feel pain instead of nothing.
To feel warm.

Warm wet colour coming
out from under his skin.
Proof of life.
Somewhere.

SARA WANDERS THESE STREETS

The boy shooting up on the street corner
is looking for exaltation, and truth
is the bag lady waltzing the grocery cart
with a giant cactus in the middle,
blooming a strawberry-gold flower
like passionfruit suckling the sky.
In an alley a girl with black moon eyes
hugs a cello with missing strings
and still some notes manage
to rise in the wind's ecstasy
and turn the afternoon almost
beautiful.

I wander these streets
in the private solitudes
made public, believing you
will appear around the next corner,
into the blooming, into the broken
song. I used to think
that sometimes something breaks
so that we can be made whole again.
But now I'm not so sure.

Beware, the heart is
a Trojan horse. And my heart
sometimes a mist
hovering the quiet pond,
sometimes a waterfall
painful and unbound,
sometimes the cage
where broken birds gather,
their small frail wings
flutter but do not fly.
Their music,
my outcry.

And what am I but
the cello aching for your arms
and the boy on the street corner
burning Rome for a moment
of fire. And the cactus spilling
its colours into the gutters
and the alleys and the cardboard boxes,
as if they might still
reach you.

Lisa Shatzky was born in Montreal, Quebec but has lived in Vancouver and Bowen Island, British Columbia for the past twenty-one years. Her poetry has been published in *The Vancouver Review, Room Magazine, Quills Canadian Poetry Magazine, The Prairie Journal, The Antigonish Review, The Dalhousie Review, Canadian Women's Studies, The Nashwaak Review, The New Quarterly*, six chapbooks edited by Patrick Lane, and many anthologies across Canada and the United States. When not writing, she works as a trauma therapist and runs marathons, kayaks, and wanders among ancient trees.

Advance Praise for *Do Not Call Me By My Name*

"Lisa Shatzky makes us pay attention in these beautiful, troubling poems. What can we take for granted after reading them? She writes of First Nations children with cirgarette burns, children who slash themselves, the nightmares they carry inside them, their pain, the pain of their wounded parents, wounded grandparents. And the ones who find their way home, " through thistles and throrns." This is an important book. Read these poems. It will change you."
— Wendy Morton, author of *Gumshoe* and *6 Impossible Things Before Breakfast*

"These poems are placed like cold steel beds lined up row upon row. Visceral. Lisa Shatzky writes in gunmetal residue—evidence bagged from Canada's largest crime scene of the Residential School era. As she opened the vaulted doors into each child's memory, she was slashed by tormented truth, laughter at lost blood, lost stories. In this collection, you'll witness bruised stones, shattered sparrow prayers, an eight-year-old playing dead, the blue above, blue below a man about to jump. All the while in the room where you read, ghost dancers' shadows emerge through thick walls. Watching blood and ink mix. Waiting to be fed. Waiting to be invited in."
— Sandra Lynn Lynxleg, child of a Residential School Survivor and District Principal of Aboriginal Education, School District 22 Vernon

'I appreciate the words Lisa Shatzky has written; it is the closest to the truth I have heard for a long time. People keep forgetting about the past, especially a past that does not belong to them. If we do not remember the past, we are destined to make those mistakes again. Thank you Lisa for making these memories available to those who would never know."
— Simon James, First Nations artist, story teller (*Raven Tales*) and carver

"These are poems of unspeakable bravery. Out of this grieving comes a spiritual renewal and hope for us all. Read them with all your heart."
— Patrick Lane, winner of the Governor General's Award for Poetry

Marquis Book Printing Inc.

Québec, Canada
2011